Beginning 1

Using Higher-Order Thinking to Improve Critical Reading and Comprehension

Inference Jones products available in print or eBook form.

Beginning 1 • Beginning 2 • Level 1

Written by
Noreen Conte

Graphic Design by
Scott Slyter

THE CRITICAL THINKING CO.™
www.CriticalThinking.com
Phone: 800-458-4849 • Fax: 541-756-1758
1991 Sherman Ave., Suite 200 • North Bend • OR 97459
ISBN 978-1-64420-002-5

Printed in the United States of America by Sheridan Books, Inc., Ann Arbor, MI (Apr. 2023)

Table of Contents

Introduction

An inference is a conclusion based on evidence and knowledge. This book teaches students what an inference is and how to make good inferences based on evidence and knowledge. It will also help students improve critical reading and higher level thinking skills. Before students begin making inferences, it is important to lead them through the brief lessons in the beginning of the book. Readers in grades one and two will become familiar with making inferences as they read.

What is an Inference

An inference is a conclusion based on evidence and knowledge. Study each picture below and read each sentence. Using what you know and what you have experienced, complete each sentence.

Example:

Rob did not go to school today, because he was not feeling well.

I know this because he has a thermometer in his mouth.

1. Paula didn't want to get ____________________ when she walked to her friend's house.

   I know this because she has an ______________________________.

2. Today is someone's ____________________________.

   I know this because ____________________________________

   ____.

3. The baby birds are waiting for their mother to

   ____________________________.

   I know this because ____________________________________

   ____.

4. It was ___________________ outside when Barb walked her dog.

   I know this because ____________________________________

   ____.

The Importance of Identifying Evidence When Making an Inference

Evidence is information that proves or helps prove a claim or statement.

Example: Mary watched her mom go into each bedroom collecting clothes in a laundry basket. Her mom always collects clothes in a laundry basket before she puts them in the washing machine.

Inference: Mary inferred that her mom was going to wash clothes.

Write **evidence** on the line before the sentence that proves or helps prove Mary's inference. Write **knowledge** on the line before the sentence that tells you something that Mary had learned.

___Knowledge___ Mary remembered that her mom always gathers clothes in a laundry basket before putting them in the washing machine.

___Evidence___ Mary watched her mom collecting clothes from each bedroom in a laundry basket.

1. Mick looked out the window and saw a boy wearing a hat, gloves, and boots. The boy was shoveling snow. Mick inferred that the boy was shoveling the driveway. Mick saw the weather had changed, and winter had arrived. Mick thought about the hat, gloves, and boots he wore in the winter when he shoveled the driveway.

Write **evidence** on the line before the sentence that proves or helps prove Mick's inference. Write **knowledge** on the line before the sentence that tells you something that Mick had learned.

________________ Mick saw a boy wearing a hat, gloves, and boots and was shoveling snow.

________________ Mick thought about the hat, gloves, and boots he wore in the winter when he shoveled the driveway.

2. Larry looked at the smiling faces of the kids on the playground playing in the sand, swinging on the swings, and sliding down the slide. Larry inferred that the children were happy to be at the playground. He thought about how happy he was when he played on the playground.

Write **evidence** on the line before the sentence that proves or helps prove Larry's inference. Write **knowledge** on the line before the sentence that tells you something Larry had learned.

__________________ Larry thought about how happy he was when he played on the playground.

__________________ Larry looked at the smiling faces of the kids on the playground playing in the sand, swinging on the swings, and sliding down the slide.

3. Nicole looked at the smiling face of the chef holding a pizza in one hand and holding a thumb up on his other hand. Nicole inferred that the chef was proud of his pizza. She remembered how she smiled when her dad gave her a thumbs-up when she scored a run in a baseball game.

Write **evidence** on the line before the sentence that proves or helps prove Nicole's inference. Write **knowledge** on the line before the sentence that tells you something that Nicole had learned.

____________________ Nicole looked at the smiling face of the chef holding a pizza in one hand and holding a thumb up on his other hand.

____________________ She remembered how she smiled when her dad gave her a thumbs-up when she scored a run in a baseball game.

Supported and Unsupported Inferences

When making an inference, you use your knowledge and any evidence you can find. For each inference below, write **supported** on the line that shows the evidence that supports the inference. Write **unsupported** on the line if the inference is not supported by the evidence.

Example: Amy noticed that Kris was yawning a lot in class.

supported ______ Amy inferred that Kris was tired or bored.

unsupported ______ Amy inferred that Kris didn't sleep at all last night.

1. Lori looked out the window on Saturday afternoon and saw the man next door rolling his lawn mower out of his garage.

    ____________________ Lori inferred that he no longer wanted to keep it in his garage.

    ____________________ Lori inferred that he was going to mow his lawn.

2. As he entered the grandstands, Jim smiled when he saw his friends cheering.

    ____________________ Jim inferred that their team was doing well.

    ____________________ Jim inferred that their team had been penalized.

3. Mom rolled out the dough and the kids helped make the tasty treats.

____________________ Mom and the kids would bake dough.

____________________ The kids are going to take the cookies to school for a party.

4. After Joe's dog ran in the mud in the backyard, Joe had to clean him up.

____________________ Joe would not let the dog play in the backyard again today.

____________________ Joe has to clean his dog up often.

5. Caroline looked outside and saw her friend, Sky, walking with an open umbrella.

____________________ It's raining outside.

____________________ The street will be flooded from the rain.

Where?

Use your knowledge and evidence to infer where each person is located in each sentence below. Find your answer in the choice box, and write it on the blank line. Each answer can only be used once.

theater	supermarket	restaurant	beach	playground
farm	school	amusement park	basketball game	library

1. Rob walked into the classroom and sat down at his desk. He took out his homework. ____________________
2. Amy stood in line waiting to ride the roller coaster. ____________________
3. Nicole walked on the sand as the waves tickled her feet. ____________________
4. Sky walked to the sixth row with her popcorn and sat down to watch the movie. ____________________
5. Kris followed his uncle to the barn to help him milk the cows. ____________________
6. Meadow picked up a bunch of bananas and put them in the shopping cart. ____________________
7. Joe smiled when the waitress brought his chocolate cream pie. ____________________
8. After Billie slid down the slide, she ran and hopped on a swing. ____________________
9. Jose sat down for story time and then checked out his books. ____________________
10. With only five seconds left in the game, the player made a basket to win the game. ____________________

Who?

Use your knowledge and evidence to infer the person's job in each sentence below. Find your answer in the choice box, and write it on the blank line. Each answer can only be used once.

principal	actor	librarian	baker	mailman	teacher
	policeman	farmer	hairdresser	gardener	

1. Mrs. Ramos said, "Boys and girls, it's time to line up for lunch." ____________________

2. "Let me help you check out your books," Miss White said. ____________________

3. Over the loudspeaker, Mr. Davis said "Because of the snowstorm, you'll be going home early today." ____________________

4. Susan said, "Come over to the sink. I'm going to wash your hair before I cut it." ____________________

5. Jim used his tractor to plow his land before he planted his crops. ____________________

6. Lori made a chocolate cake, a cherry pie, and some brownies to sell in her shop. ____________________

7. When Mr. Jackson saw a man speeding, he stopped the man and gave him a ticket. ____________________

8. After the play, Ron bowed as the people clapped for him. ____________________

9. Mr. Kelly sorted the mail before delivering it. ____________________

10. Sam was hired to cut the lawn and plant some flowers in my yard. ____________________

Feelings

Use your knowledge and evidence to infer how each person feels in each sentence below. Find your answer in the choice box, and write it on the blank line. Each answer can only be used once.

scared	frustrated	tired	proud	surprised	excited
disappointed	embarrassed	jealous	sick		

1. When the football player scored a touchdown, Sam jumped out of his seat and yelled, "Hurray!" ______________

2. After trying to solve the math problem over and over, Rosa put her head down on her desk and sighed. ______________

3. Our puppy, Sophie, started shaking when she heard the thunder. ______________

4. When Mike finally learned to ride his bike, he couldn't stop smiling. ______________

5. Grandpa said he didn't get much sleep last night. ______________

6. Larry opened his birthday present and grinned, because he didn't expect a puppy. ______________

7. The first graders knew there would be no recess when they heard the thunder. ______________

8. Barb thought it wasn't fair that her older sister was allowed to go to the movies with a friend and Barb wasn't. ______________

9. Dad took some medicine and laid down to take a nap. ______________

10. On my first day of school I needed help, but I didn't ask for it. ______________

Weather

Use your knowledge and evidence to infer the weather described in each sentence below. Find your answer in the choice box, and write it on the blank line. Each answer can only be used once.

rainy	sunny	cloudy	rainbow	thunderstorm
windy	snowy	hot	flood	cold

1. Dad was outside for a long time shoveling the driveway. ________________

2. Mom left for a walk, but after a minute, she returned to get her umbrella. ________________

3. Dan and Katie were so excited about cooling off in their friend's new pool. ________________

4. We giggled when we walked outside for recess and saw our teacher's hat fly right off her head. ________________

5. Since it was time for dismissal, the second graders put on their coats, hats, and mittens. ________________

6. The sun was shining this morning, but now it's hidden. ________________

7. The sound of the storm and the flashes of lightning scared us. ________________

8. When Carol walked out the door, she knew right away that she needed her sunglasses. ________________

9. After it rained, I looked up at the sky and saw a band of beautiful colors. ________________

10. We were afraid the heavy rain would keep pouring down and come into our house. ________________

Animals

Use your knowledge and evidence to infer what animal is mentioned in each sentence below. Find your answer in the choice box, and write it on the blank line. Each answer can only be used once.

skunk	squirrel	cat	turtle	spider	elephant
kangaroo	giraffe	bee	dog		

1. My cousin and I watched the little animal with a fluffy tail run up the tree. ________________
2. The huge, gray animal raised his trunk and made a loud noise. ________________
3. Harry ran away from the bug, because he was afraid the bug would sting him. ________________
4. When she heard meowing outside her window, Mary knew her tiny pet was in the backyard. ________________
5. The family walked quickly out of the park when they saw a small black and white animal. ________________
6. The third graders giggled when they saw the animal's head and legs go into its shell. ________________
7. My brother looked at the zoo animal and said, "Why is his neck so long?" ________________
8. I was surprised when I saw a hopping animal with a baby in its pouch. ________________
9. When I heard the barking, I knew a stranger was walking by the house. ________________
10. I looked at the animal and wondered what it would be like to have eight legs. ________________

Special Days

Use your knowledge and evidence to infer the special day described in each sentence below. Find your answer in the choice box, and write it on the blank line. Each answer can be used only once.

Thanksgiving	first day of school	Halloween	Valentine's Day
graduation	wedding	birthday	Fourth of July
last day of school	Christmas		

1. I was excited when my mom put candles on the cake and my presents on the table. ______________
2. The turkey looked yummy, but I was looking forward to the pumpkin pie. ______________
3. Kevin walked into the building hoping Mr. Loftus would be his teacher this year. ______________
4. After eating hot dogs and hamburgers, we watched the fireworks and sang "God Bless America." ______________
5. Camille walked out of her school thinking of all the fun things she would do starting tomorrow. ______________
6. "Will your mom let you go trick or treating with me today?" Mark asked Rob. ______________
7. When we walked into the living room, Maureen and I noticed that Santa had eaten the cookies we left for him. ______________
8. "I would rather get more chocolate hearts today than cards!" I told my parents. ______________
9. I couldn't believe I would become Mrs. Jackson during the ceremony today. ______________
10. Tony watched as his brother walked on stage and accepted his diploma. ______________

Games

Use your knowledge and evidence to infer the game described in ach sentence. Find your answer in the choice box, and write it on the blank line. Each answer can be used only once.

volleyball	freeze tag	hide and seek	football	soccer
basketball	baseball	hockey	kickball	dodgeball

1. The quarterback caught the pass and scored a touchdown. ______________________
2. I ran behind the garage where no one could see me. ______________________
3. When Henry touched my arm, I had to stand still. ______________________
4. Nancy hit the ball and ran around the bases to make a homerun. ______________________
5. Sammy dribbled the ball down the court. ______________________
6. The player scored a goal because the goalie couldn't stop the puck. ______________________
7. Meadow kicked the ball and scored a goal. ______________________
8. Bill ran quickly so the ball wouldn't hit him. ______________________
9. Barb kicked the ball and ran to third base. ______________________
10. Mom, Dad, and I watched as the teams hit the ball back and forth over the net. ______________________

When?

Use your knowledge and evidence to infer when each sentence is taking place. Find your answer in the choice box, and write the letter on the blank line.

a. during the day in the summer	b. during the day in the winter
c. during the night in the summer	d. during the night in the winter

1. The family sat down in the backyard to watch the fireworks. ________

2. Kevin looked up at the streetlight and saw hundreds of snowflakes falling from the sky. ________

3. Dad turned on the pool lights so we could go swimming. ________

4. Cindy, Lucy, and Mick played basketball at the playground. ________

5. After making our snowman, I asked my mom for a carrot for the snowman's nose. ________

6. My sister and I could see the snow falling in the car headlights. ________

7. My brother and I took turns spraying each other with the hose to cool off. ________

8. Tony, Jim, and Molly looked up at the sun as they made angels in the snow. ________

9. The boys and girls screamed as they slid down the hill on their sleds. ________

10. The campers sat around the campfire and sang songs. ________

What Subject?

Use your knowledge and evidence to infer what subject each sentence is about. Find your answer in the choice box, and write it on the blank line. Each answer can only be used once.

reading	math	social studies	science	geography
writing	music	phonics	art	gym class

1. Pedro studied a map of the United States to find state capitals. ______________________

2. Lori painted a picture of flowers, trees, and the blue sky. ______________________

3. Tony took out his flash cards so Dad could help him with his addition facts. ______________________

4. Cindy was having difficulty sounding out a word in her workbook. ______________________

5. The teacher told the class to read the short story and talk about the main idea. ______________________

6. For homework, the students had to write five facts about the American flag. ______________________

7. The class had to learn the names of the nine planets. ______________________

8. Coach Rob taught us how to do jumping jacks. ______________________

9. The boys and girls practiced singing songs for their program. ______________________

10. Sharon wrote a story about her first day at school. ______________________

What Will Happen Next?

Read each sentence. Below each sentence, read the three choices for your answer. Use your knowledge and evidence to infer what will happen next. Circle the sentence you have chosen.

1. Sue carried a backpack and waved as she walked out the door.
   a. The girl will go shopping.
   b. The girl will take her dog for a walk.
   c. The girl will wait for the school bus in front of her house.

2. The boy carried a trumpet down the hall at school.
   a. The boy will go to the lunchroom.
   b. The boy is on his way to band practice.
   c. The boy is going to play the trumpet at recess.

3. Two children talked and giggled at the library.
   a. The children will roll on the floor laughing.
   b. The librarian will tell them to leave the library.
   c. The librarian will remind them that the library is a quiet place.

4. The little girl walked with her dad as he pushed a shopping cart.
   a. The child will pay for the food in the cart.
   b. The child will help her dad find the food and put it in the cart.
   c. The child will taste the food.

5. A girl and a boy each carried a bucket and a shovel on the beach.
   a. The girl and boy will go jump in the waves.
   b. The girl and boy will sit under a beach umbrella.
   c. The girl and boy will make a sandcastle.

6. We saw a lady buying yarn at a craft store today.
   a. The lady will cut up the yarn and glue the pieces on a piece of paper.
   b. The lady will make a blanket to put on her bed.
   c. The lady will make a leash for her dog.

7. Three kids were each rolling a snowball to make it bigger
   a. The children will throw the big balls of snow at each other.
   b. The children will carry the huge balls of snow into the house.
   c. The children will make a snowman.

8. A girl dressed up like a witch walked down our street.
   a. The girl will run down the street scaring people.
   b. The girl will fly into the sky on her broomstick.
   c. The girl will go trick or treating.

Family

Read the words in the choice box. Each word refers to a person in the family. Read each sentence. Use your knowledge and evidence to infer a word from the choice box that could replace the **bold-faced** words. Write the word on the blank line in sentence below.

grandma	aunt	daughter	grandpa	uncle	brother
cousin	sister	mother-in-law	father-in-law		

1. My **mother's sister** took me to the movies.
   My ______________________ took me to the movies.

2. I went to the football game with my **father's brother**.
   I went to the football game with my ______________________.

3. Cindy walked to school with her **aunt's daughter**.
   Cindy walked to school with her ______________________.

4. My **father's baby boy** giggles when I tickle him.
   My ______________________ giggles when I tickle him.

5. Tom likes spending time with his **mother's father**.
   Tom likes spending time with his ______________________.

6. Sherry's **husband's father** likes to play games with the kids.
   Sherry's ______________________ likes to play games with the kids.

7. I watched cartoons with my **mom's daughter**.
   I watch cartoons with my ______________________.

8. Tom's **wife's mother** baked a cake for Tom's birthday.
   Tom's ______________________ baked a cake for Tom's birthday.

9. My **mother's mother** helps me with my homework.
   My ______________________ helps me with my homework.

10. Henry danced with his **little girl** at the wedding.
    Henry danced with his ______________________ at the wedding.

Words with More Than One Meaning

Some words have more than one meaning. Read each sentence below. Two meanings are given under the sentence. Circle the meaning of the **bold-faced** word used in the sentence.

1. George likes looking at the pretty colors of the leaves in the **fall**.
   a. to drop down from a higher place
   b. the season of autumn

2. Will you write me a **letter** when you're on vacation?
   a. a message you write and send in the mail
   b. a written mark that stands for a speech sound

3. My little sister wanted to **ring** the doorbell.
   a. a piece of jewelry worn on a finger
   b. to press a button to let your friend know you are there

4. Paula likes to **bowl** with her friends on Saturday afternoon.
   a. a deep, round dish used for holding food
   b. a game in which you roll a ball to knock down pins

5. When the rain started falling, the kids felt **blue** because there would be no recess.
   a. the color of a clear sky
   b. feeling sad or unhappy

6. Do I have to wear a **tie** to Cheryl and Sam's wedding?
   a. a strip of cloth worn around the neck
   b. to make the score even in a game or contest

7. The **pitcher** was disappointed when the batter hit the ball and got a homerun.
   a. a container holding iced tea, milk, or other liquids
   b. a baseball player who throws the ball to the batter

8. What **kind** of ice cream do you like?
   a. nice
   b. type

9. Lots of **bats** flew out from under the bridge into the sky.
   a. a small mammal that flies
   b. a club used to hit a baseball

10. Jimmy **left** his homework at his friend's house.
    a. the opposite of right
    b. to go away from a place without taking something

Words with More Than One Meaning

Some words have more than one meaning. Read each sentence below. Two meanings are given under the sentence. Circle the meaning of the **bold-faced** word used in the sentence. Use your knowledge and evidence to infer the answer.

1. I am a big **fan** of baseball and football, so I go to many games.
   a. a person who is very interested in a sports team or player
   b. a machine with blades that move to make a room cooler

2. Let's walk to the **store** and buy some ice cream.
   a. a place where things are sold
   b. to put away for future use

3. When you get to the corner, make a **right** turn.
   a. the direction opposite of left
   b. correct

4. The water slide in our yard was a big **hit** at my brother's birthday party.
   a. slap or strike
   b. something that's very popular

5. Mom uses garlic powder and oregano to **season** the meatballs.
   a. a certain part of the year
   b. to improve the flavor of something

6. Dad **leaves** for work at seven o'clock each morning.
   a. the flat parts of a tree that grow from the stem or branch
   b. to go away from a place

7. I watched as my colorful kite **rose** way into the sky.
   a. a sweet-smelling flower that comes in many colors and grows on a bush
   b. moved up in direction

8. The player picked up his **bat** and walked onto the field.
   a. a stick you use to hit a ball when playing baseball
   b. a small animal that flies at night

9. After dinner, I will **clear** the table and wash the dishes.
   a. easy to understand
   b. to move anything not wanted or in the way

10. When we left the shopping mall, we could not find our parking **space**.
   a. an area with a particular use
   b. the area that contains the universe beyond the earth

Analogies

An **analogy** shows how pairs of words go together.

Example:
Happy is to sad as up is to down.
Happy is the opposite of sad, and up is the opposite of down.

Choose a word from the choice box to complete each analogy below. Use your knowledge and evidence to infer the correct answer.

night	ocean	nose	said	soup	eyes	foot
sour	country	dark	cutting	flower	cold	fly

1. Day is to night as light is to ______________________.
2. Sand is to desert as water is to ______________________.
3. Hear is to ears as see is to ______________________.
4. Baseball is to game as rose is to ______________________.
5. Taste is to mouth as smell is to ______________________.
6. Throw is to threw as say is to ______________________.
7. Cupcake is to sweet as lemon is to ______________________.
8. Wet is to dry as hot is to ______________________.
9. Pencil is to writing as scissors are to ______________________.
10. Principal is to school as president is to ______________________.
11. Fork is to macaroni as spoon is to ______________________.
12. Sun is to day as stars are to ______________________.
13. Mitten is to hand as sock is to ______________________.
14. Fish is to swim as bird is to ______________________.

More Analogies

An **analogy** shows how pairs of words go together.

Example:

Sky is is to blue as grass is to green.
The color of the sky is blue, and the color of the grass is green.

Choose a word from the choice box to complete each analogy below. Use your knowledge and evidence to infer the correct answer.

red	scratch	smell	Dan	meow	mouse	foot
flowers	uncle	dinner	houses	dad	car	solid

1. Eyes are to see as nose is to ______________________.
2. Robert is to Rob as Daniel is to ______________________.
3. Dog is to bark as cat is to ______________________.
4. Sleepy is to yawn as itchy is to ______________________.
5. Large is to elephant as small is to ______________________.
6. Finger is to hand as toe is to ______________________.
7. Grandma is to grandpa as mom is to ______________________.
8. Closet is to clothes as garage is to ______________________.
9. Water is to liquid as ice is to ______________________.
10. Bats are to caves as people are to ______________________.
11. Noon is to lunch as evening is to ______________________.
12. Brother is to sister as aunt is to ______________________.
13. Chef is to food as florist is to ______________________.
14. Lettuce is to green as cherry is to ______________________.

The Sneeze

Read the story. Use your knowledge and evidence to infer the answers below.

Barb looked around the classroom. Most of the kids were done with their math work. Miss Jones tidied up her desk and picked up her sunglasses. Joey looked at Barb and smiled. Sure enough, Miss Jones told the students to put their math books away. She called them by rows to line up for recess. Barb was the line leader for the girls, and Joey was the line leader for the boys. Miss Jones asked Joey to close the classroom door. The class walked down the hall. They could smell spaghetti and meatballs as they passed the lunchroom.

"I can't wait for lunch! It smells yummy!" Barb whispered to Joey. When the class walked onto the playground, Miss Jones put on her sunglasses. Then she said, "Okay, boys and girls, you can go play now!"

I didn't move. Joey didn't move. No one moved.

Miss Jones said, "You can play now! Why aren't you moving?"

We just stood there. Finally, Joey said, "We're waiting for you to sneeze!"

"You're what?" the teacher said.

Suzy said, "We're waiting for you to sneeze. You always sneeze before we play unless it's a cloudy day!"

Sure enough, Miss Jones sneezed a loud sneeze. She grinned from ear to ear.

"You know me well!" she said.

When Miss Jones stopped giggling, she said, "Okay, now it's time to play!" Barb laughed. She waved to Miss Jones as she ran to play. Then, all the the kids started waving to their teacher with smiles on their faces.

1. Joey smiled at Barb because he knew it was time for ________________.

2. Write the sentence that helps you infer that the students have not eaten lunch yet.

   ____

3. Write the sentence that helps you infer that the teacher does not sneeze every day at recess.

   ____

4. Miss Jones is (angry, sad, or surprised) when the kids wait for her to sneeze.

5. You infer that the students are happy as they run to play, because they had

   ____

6. You infer that it's a sunny day, because Miss Jones took her

   ______________________________ with her when she left the classroom.

The County Fair

Read the story. Use your knowledge and evidence to infer the answers below.

Last Saturday, Mom, Dad, and I went to the county fair. We played games, ate cotton candy, and went on rides. Mom went on the roller coaster with me. It was so much fun, but it was scary, too. Dad likes the merry-go-round. All three of us sat on horses that went up and down as the merry-go-round went around and around. We smiled and laughed. Next, I wanted to go on the umbrella ride.

"Dad, please go on the umbrella ride with me! It's so much fun!" I said.

"Sure, Suzy!" he replied.

Mom said, "Rob, are you sure you want to go on that ride?"

"Yes, Jane! I'm sure!" Dad said.

The seats on the ride were like swings, and the ride went round and round up in the air. I looked at the people walking around on the ground. They looked tiny. I looked at my dad.

"What a fantastic ride!" I said as we went up in the air.

All of a sudden, my dad yelled, "Stop this ride! Stop this ride now!"

The fair worker stopped the ride so that my dad and I could get off. My dad's face was pale, and he looked kind of sad.

When we got off the ride, the fair worker looked at me and said, "Honey, are you okay?" I rolled my eyes and said, "Yes, I'm fine!"

My mom was waiting for us. She looked at my dad and shook her head.

"Mom, I think next time you should go on that ride with me."

Dad, Mom, and I looked at each other and laughed.

1. Write what Mom says that helps you infer that she thinks Dad won't like the umbrella ride.

   ____

2. The fair worker thought that ____________________________ was scared and wanted to get off the ride.

3. Suzy rolled her eyes when the worker said "Honey, are you okay?" because

   ____

4. You can infer that the umbrella ride went way up in the air because the people on the ground looked ____________________.

5. Mom shook her head when Suzy and Dad got off the ride because ____________

   ____.

Mick

Read the story. Use your knowledge and evidence to infer the answers below.

Our new puppy, Mick, is black and white, and he fits in my backpack. He's a happy dog, and he makes us laugh. If you ask him a question, he tilts his head. He always does this when you start a question with "Mick, do you want to...?"

Mick spends a lot of time looking out the windows. He also wanders around the house looking at everything. Sometimes, we have to search for him. My little sister, Sherry, likes looking for Mick when he hides. One day, Mom, Dad, Sherry, and I went to the beach for the day.

When we got home, Mick jumped up and down. He ran to each one of us so we would pet him. Then, he sniffed our beach towels and our beach bags. After being at the beach, we all needed showers. We took turns using the bathrooms. When I was finished with my shower, I went into the kitchen to help Mom with dinner.

Sherry came in the kitchen and asked me, "Sam, do you know where my teddy bears are?" I told Sherry that I hadn't seen her teddy bears for a long time. "What about my little race cars? Have you seen them?" I asked. "No, Sam!" Sherry said.

Mom and Dad looked at each other. Mom said, "My tiny pillows from the living room are missing." Dad's eyes got big. He said, "Sherry, where is your cozy blanket?"

Sherry said, "You mean my baby blanket? I don't know!"

"Wait a minute! "Where's Mick?" Dad said. We looked and looked but couldn't find him. "He really likes your room, Mom and Dad, so let's look there!" I said.

We walked into the bedroom and looked around. "No Mick!" I said. Then, I saw a black and white tail sticking out from under Mom's side of the bed. We peeked under the bed. Mick was curled up on the missing blanket. He rested his head on one of the missing pillows. Sherry's teddy bears and my race cars were scattered around Mick.

"Look! Mick has his own apartment under the bed!" Sherry said. We all giggled. Now, when something is missing, Mom says, "Be sure you look in Mick's apartment!"

1. The reader infers that Mick is curious because he ______________________________

____.

2. When the family returned home from the beach, Mick jumped up and down and wanted everyone to pet him. Mick showed that he is ______________________ to see the family.

3. ______________________ probably likes to play hide and seek because

____.

4. I think Mick is a small dog because ______________________________.

5. I know Mick is comfortable under Mom's bed because ______________________

____.

Which Store?

Use your knowledge and evidence to infer where each person is located in each sentence below. Find your answer in the choice box, and write it on the blank line. Each answer can only be used once.

shoe store	bakery	drugstore	pet store
bookstore	sporting goods store	toy store	florist
grocery store	department store		

1. Mother's Day is tomorrow, and Jimmy wants to buy flowers for his mom. ____________________

2. Kelly's nose is stuffy. She needs to buy some medicine to help her feel better. ____________________

3. Dad is planning to plant flowers in the backyard and wants to read about the different kinds of flowers. ____________________

4. Sharon needs sneakers to wear when she plays baseball with her friends. ____________________

5. Mom needs a new dress to wear to her daughter's wedding. ____________________

6. For my birthday, I'd like the chocolate chip cookie cake we saw at the mall last week. ____________________

7. Dad and Mom finally agreed that we should get a puppy. ____________________

8. My older sister, Rosa, wants to buy high heels to wear to the prom. ____________________

9. I have to go shopping for everything I need to make the Thanksgiving dinner. ____________________

10. I want to buy a game to play with my friends when they spend the night. ____________________

Field Trip

Use your knowledge and evidence to infer where each person is located in each sentence below. Find your answer in the choice box, and write it on the blank line. Each answer can only be used once.

bakery	science museum	farm	aquarium	zoo	art museum
planetarium	fire station	police station	post office		

1. "I'm looking forward to seeing all the monkeys!" said Caroline. ______________________

2. The tiny cupcakes they gave us were yummy. ______________________

3. "Seeing the dinosaur skeletons will be awesome!" Paula said. ______________________

4. Steven said, "I hope they will let us milk the cows." ______________________

5. Andy told his teacher, "I can't wait for the field trip today, because I love to paint!" ______________________

6. Lori said, "The sirens on the trucks are so loud that they scare me!" ______________________

7. "I hope I see an octopus on our field trip today!" Carol said. ______________________

8. Charlie said, "My brother and I love to look at the sky, the sun, the moon, and the stars, so I think the field trip will be fantastic!" ______________________

9. After the field trip today I wish they'd let us deliver some mail to people's houses!" Julie said. ______________________

10. "I wonder if we'll see a jail today!" my best friend said. ______________________

What Will Happen Next?

Read each sentence. Use your knowledge and evidence to infer what will happen next. Choose your answer from the choice box.

shoe store	library	theater	high school	elementary school
park	playground	airplane	dentist	principal

1. Josh closed his eyes and imagined looking out the window at the blue sky below.
   Josh is going on an ____________________.

2. Peggy had been waiting for so long to see this funny movie about a family with five dogs.
   Peggy is going to the ____________________.

3. Bob and Sandy packed a lunch and found a blanket to use for their picnic.
   They're going to the ____________________.

4. For the past couple of days Tom brushed his teeth and flossed carefully.
   Tom is going to the ____________________ soon.

5. Two third grade boys were fighting in the lunchroom.
   Now, they are on their way to see the ____________________.

6. Lori looked at her books and saw that they were overdue.
   Lori will ask her mother to drive her to the ____________________.

7. Mike's mom looked at his sneakers and said, "Those sneakers are worn out. You can't wear them to gym class."
   Mike and his mom will make a trip to a ____________________.

8. Suzy gathered all her school supplies and looked forward to going to third grade.
   Soon, Suzy will get on the bus and go to her ____________________.

9. Rosie couldn't wait to go down the slide and swing on the swings.
   Rosie and her dad are going to go to the ____________________.

10. Mark and Sally hoped that the teenagers at their new school would be friendly.
    Mark and Sally are going to a ____________________.

Idioms

Read each sentence below. In each sentence, an idiom is **bold-faced**. An idiom is a phrase that cannot be understood from the meaning of each of its words. For example, if people need to be quiet, you could tell them to **zip their lips**. You don't mean use a zipper. You mean they should be quiet. Read each sentence. Choose a meaning from the choice box for each idiom. Use your knowledge and evidence to infer the answer.

eat too much	get very angry	watch closely	easy
raining hard	give away the secret	help me	kidding me
	try to do too much	costs a lot	

1. We couldn't go in our pool, because it was **raining cats and dogs**. ______________

2. Mom said, "We can't buy that bike because it **costs an arm and a leg**." ______________

3. I hope Dad won't **blow his top** when he sees the flat tire. ______________

4. Billy said, "Don't **pig out** on snacks, because we're eating dinner soon." ______________

5. Sharon walked out of class smiling because her math test **was a piece of cake**. ______________

6. Dad said, "Would you **keep an eye** on your little sister while I get the mail?" ______________

7. Gail said, "Would someone **lend me a hand** clearing off this table?" ______________

8. When Joe said he saw a monkey in our backyard, I said "You're **pulling my leg**!" ______________

9. "Don't **bite off more than you can chew**!" Mom said when I signed up for six clubs. ______________

10. We planned a surprise for Mom. Dad said, "**Don't let the cat out of the bag**!" ______________

More Idioms

Read each sentence below. In each sentence, an idiom is **bold-faced**. An idiom is a phrase that cannot be understood from the meaning of each of its words. For example, if people need to be quiet, you could tell them to **zip their lips**. You don't mean use a zipper. You mean they should be quiet. Read each sentence. Choose a meaning from the choice box for each idiom. Use your knowledge and evidence to infer the answer.

listened carefully	bother me	very funny	wait a minute	happy
was scared	I didn't belong	agree	confusing	the rest is up to you

1. I didn't let my brother's teasing **get my goat**. ____________

2. The movie with a huge mouse and a tiny elephant was a **barrel of laughs**. ____________

3. When I made a basket to win the game, I was **walking on air**. ____________

4. I was going to dive into the pool, but I **got cold feet**. ____________

5. On the first day at my new school, I felt like **a fish out of water**. ____________

6. When the teacher was telling us about our field trip, we **were all ears**. ____________

7. The book written in Spanish was **mumbo jumbo** to me. ____________

8. My father and I didn't **see eye to eye** about my bedtime. ____________

9. I helped you study for your test so now **the ball's in your court**. ____________

10. As I walked out the door before finishing my homework, my mom said, "**Hold your horses**!" ____________

Anagrams

An **anagram** is a word made by rearranging the letters of another word. For example, **bowl** is an anagram of **blow**. In each sentence below, one word is **bold-faced**. The bold-faced words do not make sense in the sentences. In each sentence, rearrange the letters in the bold-faced word to form another word. Use your knowledge and evidence to infer the answers. Write the word in the blank.

Example: My little sister took a long **pan** this afternoon. nap

1. The teacher told us to **silent** carefully to the directions. ____________
2. We drove seven **limes** to the basketball court. ____________
3. Sam got a big **ring** on his face when he won the game. ____________
4. I like to help Mom **beak** chocolate chip cookies. ____________
5. Dad likes coffee, but Mom likes **ate**. ____________
6. I have to eat my **apes** even though I don't like them. ____________
7. We planted a pretty **lamp** tree by our pool. ____________
8. Lions, panthers, and tigers are types of **acts**. ____________
9. My **Tuna** Nancy taught me how to swim. ____________
10. The beautiful **shore** galloped to the finish line. ____________
11. I need to **dusty** my spelling words for the test. ____________
12. **Heart** is the name of our planet. ____________
13. Watch Danny **bowl** out the candles on his cake! ____________
14. The baby birds waited in their **sent** for food. ____________

More Anagrams

An **anagram** is a word made by rearranging the letters of another word. For example, **bowl** is an anagram of **blow**. In each sentence below, one word is **bold-faced**. The bold-faced words do not make sense in the sentences. In each sentence, rearrange the letters in the bold-faced word to form another word. Use your knowledge and evidence to infer the answers. Write the word in the blank.

1. The **cheater** said, "Open your math book to page ten." ____________
2. We planted roses in our **danger**. ____________
3. The beautiful **rats** twinkled in the night sky. ____________
4. Did you **dusty** for tomorrow's spelling test? ____________
5. The **low** hooted in the huge oak tree. ____________
6. The **break** made my mother's birthday cake. ____________
7. Florida is the name of our **taste**. ____________
8. I'd like to know **how** took the last piece of fudge. ____________
9. Barb had to wear her **taco** on the snowy day. ____________
10. I took out the **beard** to make a sandwich. ____________
11. Make sure you **pots** at the red light. ____________
12. We cheered for our **meat** at the basketball game. ____________
13. Ellen and I like to **steak** on the sidewalk. ____________
14. The class **stove** for class president next week. ____________
15. All the kids were quiet during **listen** reading. ____________
16. My **bus** sandwich was yummy. ____________

Synonyms

Synonyms are words that have the same or nearly the same meaning. For example, tiny and small are synonyms. In each sentence below, choose a word from the choice box that is a synonym of the **bold-faced word**. Use your knowledge and evidence to infer the answer. Write the synonym on the blank line.

Example: The movie we saw today was **great**. wonderful

large	close	fantastic	happy	bunny	giggling	tardy	smart
difficult	noisy	garbage	incorrect	collect	fast	begin	

1. I helped Dad take out the **trash** this morning. ____________
2. Michael was **late** for school because he missed the bus. ____________
3. I couldn't stop **laughing** at the funny movie. ____________
4. Make sure you **shut** the door when you leave! ____________
5. The second graders' play will **start** at two o'clock P.M. ____________
6. Would you rather have a tiny dog or a **big** dog? ____________
7. Tom thought his answer on the test was **wrong**. ____________
8. We walked **quickly** so we wouldn't be late. ____________
9. The lightning was bright, and the thunder was **loud**. ____________
10. The winner of the spelling bee was very **clever**. ____________
11. Our trip to Disneyland was **wonderful**. ____________
12. Nancy was so **glad** to see her best friend. ____________
13. The cute **rabbit** hopped around in our backyard. ____________
14. The peanut butter jar was **hard** to open. ____________
15. Please **gather** your crayons and put them in the box. ____________

More Synonyms

Synonyms are words that have the same or nearly the same meaning. For example, tiny and small are synonyms. In each sentence below, choose a word from the choice box that is a synonym of the **bold-faced word**. Use your knowledge and evidence to infer the answer. Write the synonym on the blank line.

hurry	cold	journey	beautiful	tasty	eager	leave	
simple	walk	finish	crying	sick	store	nearly	cut

1. The garden was full of **pretty** wildflowers. ____________________
2. I'll **slice** the tomatoes to put on the hamburgers. ____________________
3. When you're ready to **exit**, use the door on the left. ____________________
4. Sally started **weeping** as she watched the sad movie. ____________________
5. Ron wanted to go to the pet **shop** to look at puppies. ____________________
6. Let's **end** this game, because it's getting late. ____________________
7. My grandma likes to take a **stroll** around the park. ____________________
8. The math test was **easy**, but it was very long. ____________________
9. Donna missed school today, because she was **ill**. ____________________
10. My family and I are taking a **trip** to the Grand Canyon. ____________________
11. Mom baked a **yummy** chocolate cream pie. ____________________
12. You need to wear a coat, because it's **chilly** outside. ____________________
13. I'm **almost** finished with my homework. ____________________
14. We have plenty of time, so don't **rush**. ____________________
15. I was **excited** to see the movie. ____________________

Antonyms

Antonyms are opposites. For example, **happy** is the opposite of **sad**. In each sentence below, the **bold-faced word** doesn't make sense. Choose an antonym from the choice box that would make sense. Write the antonym on the line. Use your knowledge and evidence to infer the answer.

cloudy	smiled	close	found	awake	sweet	winter	down
winners	laughed	noisy	messy	right	dry	remembered	

1. I was glad I **forgot** my homework. ____________________
2. **Summer** is fun when I make a snowman. ____________________
3. Jimmy **frowned** when he made a homerun. ____________________
4. The park was **quiet** with the kids yelling and laughing. ____________________
5. With all the toys on the floor, my room looked so **neat**. ____________________
6. On **sunny** days, we wish for the sun to come out. ____________________
7. My job is to **wet** the dishes after Mom washes them. ____________________
8. I was happy I got all the answers **wrong**. ____________________
9. I **cried** so hard at the funny movie. ____________________
10. I'm glad I'm **asleep**, because I don't want to be late. ____________________
11. The crowd clapped for the **losers**. ____________________
12. The yummy cherries tasted so **sour**. ____________________
13. Pablo smiled when he **lost** his homework. ____________________
14. Nicky was sad when her kite fell **up** to the ground. ____________________
15. Bob walks to school, because his school is **far**. ____________________

More Antonyms

Antonyms are opposites. For example, **happy** is the opposite of **sad**. In each sentence below, the **bold-faced word** doesn't make sense. Choose an antonym from the choice box that would make sense. Write the antonym on the line. Use your knowledge and evidence to infer the answer.

best	hot	tall	loud	outdoor	throw	polite
over	light	brother	dark	crooked	fix	full

1. I'm wearing my shorts, because it's **cold** outside. __________________
2. Football and baseball are **indoor** games. __________________
3. The **rude** child said please and thank you. __________________
4. The pitcher will **catch** the ball to the batter. __________________
5. The **quiet** thunder scared all the children. __________________
6. The box was so **heavy** it was easy to carry. __________________
7. My **sister** plays on the high school football team. __________________
8. My **worst** day was the day I won the spelling bee. __________________
9. After we shopped for food, our pantry was **empty**. __________________
10. Michael was so **short** he could reach the top shelf. __________________
11. When Sue saw the **straight** picture, she frowned. __________________
12. We had to go in the house when it got **light** outside. __________________
13. Uncle Pat tried to **break** the broken bike. __________________
14. I threw the ball in the air, and it went **under** the fence. __________________

Homophones

Homophones are words that sound the same, but are spelled differently and have different meanings. For example, **for** and **four** are spelled differently and have different meanings. I waited **for** you to call me. My little sister is **four** years old. Use your knowledge and evidence to infer which word belongs in each sentence below. Write the correct word on the line.

1. I don't know ___________________ I left my spelling book. (**wear**, **where**)
2. My puppy wags his ___________________ when I pet him. (**tail**, **tale**)
3. Joey waited for his ___________________ to take him to the movies. (**ant**, **aunt**)
4. Do you think that ___________________ is a daisy? (**flour**, **flower**)
5. Please speak up, because I cannot ___________________ you. (**hear**, **here**)
6. We watched when Kelly ___________________ out the candles. (**blue**, **blew**)
7. Mom says it's not polite to ___________________ at people. (**stare**, **stair**)
8. We were so excited when we ___________________ the game. (**one**, **won**)
9. I like walking on the beach in my ___________________ feet. (**bare**, **bear**)
10. I'm going to ___________________ my friends at the playground. (**meat**, **meet**)
11. The ___________________ of twenty and twenty is forty. (**sum**, **some**)
12. ___________________ book should I read first? (**Witch**, **Which**)
13. The ___________________ finished cleaning at four o'clock. (**maid**, **made**)
14. Sue didn't know ___________________ to rest or go outside. (**whether**, **weather**)
15. You have ___________________ so much since last summer. (**groan**, **grown**)

More Homophones

Homophones are words that sound the same, but are spelled differently and have different meanings. For example, **for** and **four** are spelled differently and have different meanings. I waited **for** you to call me. My little sister is **four** years old. Use your knowledge and evidence to infer which word belongs in each sentence below. Write the correct word on the line.

1. I will be ____________________ years old tomorrow. (**ate**, **eight**)
2. Do you ____________________ the names of the nine planets? (**know**, **no**)
3. Our car wouldn't start, so a man had to _________________ it away. (**toe**, **tow**)
4. We dug a ____________________ in our yard so we could plant a tree. (**hole**, **whole**)
5. "Should ___________________ pack my suitcase for the trip?" I asked. (**eye**, **I**)
6. The team cheered when they __________________ the soccer game. (**won**, **one**)
7. Janet tried to untie the ____________________ in her shoe laces. (**not**, **knot**)
8. Will you ___________________ to me when you're away at camp? (**right**, **write**)
9. In class, I had to read ____________________ from my math book. (**aloud**, **allowed**)
10. The airplane flew _____________________ into the sky. (**high**, **hi**)
11. Mom says I always ____________________ when it's time for bed. (**grown**, **groan**)
12. Lee asked his mom to ____________________ him new sneakers. (**by**, **buy**)
13. Would you like a bowl of ____________________ for lunch? (**chilly**, **chili**)
14. I watched the ship ____________________ across the lake. (**sail**, **sale**)
15. Did you know a basement is also called a ___________________? (**seller**, **cellar**)

Rhyming Words

Rhyming words are words that end with the same sound. For example, **ball** and **tall** are rhyming words. They end with the same sound. For each word below, write three rhyming words. Use your knowledge and evidence to infer each answer.

Example: ball ____tall____, ____small____, ____call____

1. hat ________, ________, ________
2. sing ________, ________, ________
3. mad ________, ________, ________
4. show ________, ________, ________
5. day ________, ________, ________
6. can ________, ________, ________
7. bake ________, ________, ________
8. glide ________, ________, ________
9. school ________, ________, ________
10. chip ________, ________, ________
11. jet ________, ________, ________
12. tack ________, ________, ________
13. run ________, ________, ________
14. well ________, ________, ________
15. kick ________, ________, ________

More Rhyming Words

Rhyming words are words that end with the same sound. For example, **sit** and **hit** are rhyming words. For each sentence below, fill in the blanks with two rhyming words from the choice box that make sense in the sentence. Use your knowledge and evidence to infer your answers.

Example: I wanted to **bake** a **cake** for my sister's birthday.

frog	snowing	toy	vet	room	brother	fat		
mouse	crawl	chick	sunny	cat	hall	blowing	fun	boy
house	pick	pet	bunny	broom	mother	sun	log	

1. One ________________ day, I saw a ________________ hopping in the park.

2. Al watched the baby ________________ down the ________________.

3. Mom got the ______________ so she could sweep the ________________.

4. Look at the ________________ sitting on that ________________.

5. My ________________ and ________________ smiled when they saw me.

6. When it was ________________, the wind was ________________.

7. The ________________ couldn't wait to play with his new ________________.

8. Tom said, "I think we have a ________________ in our ________________!"

9. The ________________ ________________ ran after the rat.

10. I wanted to ________________ up the little ________________.

11. My tiny dog wouldn't eat or play, so I took my ________________ to the ________________.

12. Let's go to the beach and have ______________ in the ________________.

Outside to Play on a Snowy Day

Read the story. Use your knowledge and evidence to infer the answers below.

The snow started falling in the morning. First, it covered the grass like a white blanket. Danny and I watched the snow pile up deeper and deeper. Mom was talking on the phone. We waited for her to finish her call.

When she finished talking she said, "I know you want to play outside, but you have to finish cleaning your room." Danny and I picked up all the toys on the floor of our room and put them away. We both made our beds. We put on our coats, mittens, hats, and boots. I found a big hat, a yellow scarf, a carrot, two big blue buttons, and seven small red buttons. Mom opened the door and we walked out. She smiled and said, "Maybe you'll be done making your snowman by the time your dad gets home!"

Danny said, "Larry, I think you should make the bottom of the snowman, because you're bigger than me. I'll start with the head!"

"Okay!" I said. "Remember to make a snowball, and then roll it in the snow to make it bigger."

It didn't take Danny long to make the head. I told him to make sure it was big enough to use the two big buttons, the carrot, and seven tiny buttons for the face.

I kept rolling and rolling my snowball to make it bigger. He made a snowball and rolled it around to make the middle of the snowman. When we finished rolling, we put the huge ball of snow in front of the house. Then, we lifted the medium-sized ball of snow on top of that. Then, we put the small snowball on the very top.

"Good job!" I said to Danny. Danny smiled and hugged our snowman.

I put the big hat on the snowman's head, and Danny wrapped the scarf around the snowman's neck. We used the two large blue buttons, the carrot, and the seven small red buttons to make the snowman's face. Danny made the mouth into a frown.

"Hey! Danny!" I said. "Do you really want a sad snowman in our front yard?"

Danny said, "No. I just wanted to see if I could make him look really sad and I did!" Then, he moved the buttons to make a huge smile on the snowman's face!

"Fantastic!" I said.

Danny said, "Look! Dad's home! Let's show Mom and Dad our frozen friend!"

1. I think this story takes place in the (spring, summer, winter, fall) because

   ____.

2. Mom is at home, and I think Dad is probably at ____________________.

3. Larry and Danny are probably brothers, because ______________________

   ____.

4. The boys used the two big buttons for the snowman's ________________.

5. They used the carrot for the ____________________.

6. Danny and Larry used the small buttons for the snowman's ______________.

Answers

Page 1

1. wet
   umbrella
2. birthday
   I see a birthday cake and balloons
3. feed them
   the mom has a worm and the baby birds have their mouths open
4. windy
   Barb's hair is blowing in the wind

Page 2

1. evidence, knowledge

Page 3

2. knowledge, evidence
3. evidence, knowledge

Page 4

1. unsupported
   supported
2. supported
   unsupported

Page 5

3. supported
   unsupported
4. supported
   unsupported
5. supported
   unsupported

Page 6

1. school
2. amusement park
3. beach
4. theater
5. farm
6. supermarket
7. restaurant
8. playground
9. library
10. basketball game

Page 7

1. teacher
2. librarian
3. principal
4. hairdresser
5. farmer
6. baker
7. policeman
8. actor
9. mailman
10. gardener

Page 8

1. excited
2. frustrated
3. scared
4. proud
5. tired
6. surprised
7. disappointed
8. jealous
9. sick
10. embarrassed

Page 9

1. snowy
2. rainy
3. hot
4. windy
5. cold
6. cloudy
7. thunderstorm
8. sunny
9. rainbow
10. flood

Page 10

1. squirrel
2. elephant
3. bee
4. cat
5. skunk
6. turtle
7. giraffe
8. kangaroo
9. dog
10. spider

Page 11

1. birthday
2. Thanksgiving
3. first day of school
4. Fourth of July
5. last day of school

6. Halloween
7. Christmas
8. Valentine's Day
9. wedding
10. graduation

Page 12
1. football
2. hide and seek
3. freeze tag
4. baseball
5. basketball
6. hockey
7. soccer
8. dodgeball
9. kickball
10. volleyball

Page 13
1. c
2. d
3. c
4. a
5. b
6. d
7. a
8. b
9. b
10. c

Page 14
1. geography
2. art
3. math
4. phonics
5. reading
6. social studies
7. science
8. gym class
9. music
10. writing

Page 15
1. c. The girl will wait for the school bus in front of her house.
2. b. The boy is on his way to band practice.
3. c. The librarian will remind them that the library is a quiet place.
4. b. The child will help her dad find the food and put it in the cart.
5. c. The girl and boy will make a sandcastle.
6. b. The lady will make a blanket to put on her bed.
7. c. The children will make a snowman.
8. c. The girl will go trick or treating.

Page 16
1. aunt
2. uncle
3. cousin
4. brother
5. grandpa
6. father-in-law
7. sister
8. mother-in-law
9. grandma
10. daughter

Page 17
1. b. the season of autumn
2. a. a message you write and send it in the mail
3. b. to press a doorbell to let your friend know you are there
4. b. a game in which you roll a ball to knock down pins
5. b. sad or unhappy
6. a. a strip of cloth worn around the neck
7. b. a baseball player who throws the ball to the batter
8. b. type
9. a. a small mammal that flies
10. b. to go away from a place without taking something

Page 18
1. a. a person who is very interested in a sports team or player
2. a. a place where things are sold
3. a. the opposite of left
4. b. something that's very popular
5. b. to improve the flavor of something
6. b. to go away from a place
7. b. moved up in direction
8. a. a stick you use to hit a ball when playing baseball
9. b. to move anything not wanted
10. a. an area with a particular use

Page 19

1. dark
2. ocean
3. eyes
4. flower
5. nose
6. said
7. sour
8. cold
9. cutting
10. country
11. soup
12. night
13. foot
14. fly

Page 20

1. smell
2. Dan
3. meow
4. scratch
5. mouse
6. foot
7. dad
8. car
9. solid
10. houses
11. dinner
12. uncle
13. flowers
14. red

Page 21

1. recess
2. "I can't wait for lunch!"
3. "You always sneeze before we play unless it's a cloudy day!"
4. surprised
5. smiles on their faces
6. sunglasses

Page 22

1. "Rob, are you sure you want to go on that ride?"
2. Suzy
3. her dad was the one who was scared
4. tiny
5. she knew Dad wouldn't like the umbrella ride

Page 23

1. looks out the windows and wanders around the house looking at everything
2. happy
3. Mick – he likes to hide under the bed
4. he fits in Sam's backpack
5. he was curled up on a blanket with his head on a pillow

Page 24

1. florist
2. drugstore
3. bookstore
4. sporting goods store
5. department store
6. bakery
7. pet store
8. shoe store
9. grocery store
10. toy store

Page 25

1. zoo
2. bakery
3. science museum
4. farm
5. art museum
6. fire station
7. aquarium
8. planetarium
9. post office
10. police station

Page 26

1. airplane
2. theater
3. park
4. dentist
5. principal
6. library
7. shoe store
8. elementary school
9. playground
10. high school

Page 27

1. raining hard
2. costs a lot
3. get very angry

4. eat too much
5. easy
6. watch closely
7. help me
8. kidding me
9. try to do too much
10. give away the secret

Page 28
1. bother me
2. very funny
3. happy
4. was scared
5. I didn't belong
6. listened carefully
7. confusing
8. agree
9. the rest is up to you
10. wait a minute

Page 29
1. listen
2. miles
3. grin
4. bake
5. tea
6. peas
7. palm
8. cats
9. Aunt
10. horse
11. study
12. Earth
13. blow
14. nest

Page 30
1. teacher
2. garden
3. star
4. study
5. owl
6. baker
7. state
8. who
9. coat
10. bread
11. stop
12. team
13. skate
14. votes
15. silent
16. sub

Page 31
1. garbage
2. tardy
3. giggling
4. close
5. begin
6. large
7. incorrect
8. fast
9. noisy
10. smart
11. fantastic
12. happy
13. bunny
14. difficult
15. collect

Page 32
1. beautiful
2. cut
3. leave
4. crying
5. store
6. finish
7. walk
8. simple
9. sick
10. journey
11. tasty
12. cold
13. nearly
14. hurry
15. eager

Page 33
1. remembered
2. winter
3. smiled
4. noisy
5. messy
6. cloudy
7. dry
8. right
9. laughed
10. awake
11. winners
12. sweet
13. found

14. down
15. close

Page 34

1. hot
2. outdoor
3. polite
4. throw
5. loud
6. light
7. brother
8. best
9. full
10. tall
11. crooked
12. dark
13. fix
14. over

Page 35

1. where
2. tail
3. aunt
4. flower
5. hear
6. blew
7. stare
8. won
9. bare
10. meet
11. sum
12. Which
13. maid
14. whether
15. grown

Page 36

1. eight
2. know
3. tow
4. hole
5. I
6. won
7. knot
8. write
9. aloud
10. high
11. groan
12. buy
13. chili
14. sail
15. cellar

Page 37

Answers will vary.
Possible answers:

1. cat, bat, rat
2. wing, ring, thing
3. glad, sad, bad
4. snow, glow, blow
5. stay, play, clay
6. man, plan, ran
7. lake, cake, shake
8. slide, ride, hide
9. fool, cool, pool
10. dip, hip, ship
11. pet, wet, net
12. snack, stack, pack
13. fun, stun, bun
14. spell, smell, yell
15. click, stick, brick

Page 38

1. sunny, bunny
2. crawl, hall
3. broom, room
4. frog, log
5. mother, brother
6. snowing, blowing
7. boy, toy
8. mouse, house
9. fat, cat
10. pick, chick
11. pet, vet
12. fun, sun

Page 39

1. winter – it's cold outside and it's snowing
2. work
3. they have the same room *or* Danny said, "Let's show Mom and Dad our frozen friend!"
4. eyes
5. nose
6. mouth